AWA 1

HOW TO DRINK A

'This elegantly written, information-stuffed book will give
hours of pleasure'
Warwick Roger, *North & South*

'An unpretentious little gem that will sit happily on
wine lovers' shelves'
Anna McIntyre, *Marlborough Saturday Express*

'If you love wine and love reading, you will love this book'
Sue Courtney, *www.wineoftheweek.com*

'Saker writes about wine in a way that makes you long for
whatever it was that he's had'
Margo White, *Metro*

'However much you know about wine, this book is a must'
Terry Dunleavy, *New Zealand Wine Grower*

'Saker's prose is distinctly dashing for an ex-ball player –
liberally sprinkled with lively and often spicy anecdotes. This is
just one in a series of books ... I might have to buy the lot'
Charles Gill, *Taranaki Daily News*

'Witty and bright, vigorous and exciting ... The anecdotes
are funny, the information useful – this book is worth every cent'
Kate Fraser, *The Press*

'A wonderfully witty and well-researched book by a
Kiwi who certainly knows his wine'
Michelle Chilton, *Mirror*

'John Saker offers the vigorous and exciting sensations we expect
from top wines and top wine books. Brimming with entertaining
anecdote, *How to Drink a Glass of Wine* will be a happy top-up
to the wine-lover's bookshelf'
Martin Brown, www.wine-searcher.com

05

THE GINGER SERIES

how to drink a glass of wine

john saker

AWA PRESS

First edition published in 2005 by
Awa Press, PO Box 11-416,
Wellington, New Zealand

Reprinted 2006, 2007

National Library of New Zealand Cataloguing-in-Publication Data
Saker, John.
How to drink a glass of wine / John Saker. 1st ed.
(The ginger series ; 5)
ISBN 0-9582538-2-X
1. Wine and wine making—New Zealand. I. Title. II. Series.
641.220993—dc 22

Typeset by Jill Livestre, Archetype
Printed by Printlink, Wellington
Printed on environmentally friendly and chlorine-free Munken paper.
This book is typeset in Walbaum

www.awapress.com

For my mother,
Gay Saker

ALSO BY JOHN SAKER

Tracing the Arc

ABOUT THE AUTHOR

JOHN SAKER started his working life as a professional basketball player in France, after university study in New Zealand and the United States. In 1984 he took up a career in journalism and since 1990 has worked freelance. His features and columns have appeared in many publications, including *New Zealand Listener*, *North & South*, *National Business Review*, *Southern Skies*, *The Dominion Post*, *Capital Times* and the *Weekend Herald's Canvas* magazine. In 2002 he won the Cathay Pacific Travel Writing Award. In 2007 he became *Cuisine* magazine's New Zealand wine writer.

The rich

want

good wine;

the poor

Goethe *a lot of wine.*

In a French vineyard

EVERY TIME I looked up, Marie-Thérèse's backside eclipsed the view. It was always moving away from me, the pacesetter in a plodding patrol of backsides.

Bending double was the best way − or, more to the point, the least painful way − to attack the stout, un-trellised Provençal vines and strip them of their small dark orbs of juice. 'Back-breaking work' was, for once, the perfect description. If I stopped and unfolded I could temporarily tranquillise my angry spine, but I would also fall behind.

Marie-Thérèse and her friends travelled down the

vine rows like intent pecking hens among spilled seed. Trying to close the gap if their lead became embarrassing meant really stepping on the gas, and that held the potential for pain of a different sort. My left hand still carries traces of hurried misjudged lunges with those secateurs.

We were a work gang of two hemispheres: six New Zealanders – three young couples not long out of university – and the rest mostly 60- and 70-something women from Flayosc, the nearby *village perché* that overlooked most of the vineyards in which we worked. The church bells of Flayosc dictated the shape of our working days.

Marie-Thérèse was the *grande dame* of Flayoscais grape-pickers. Her father had perished in the human abattoir of Verdun over 50 years earlier, and she had probably worked more vintages in these fields than anybody. She was hard-working, and shockingly provincial in outlook. When we shared our enthusiasm for someone we thought was a French cultural treasure, Marie-Thérèse cut the conversation short. 'Piaf? She was nothing but a prostitute.'

Yet behind the narrowed, assessing gaze and blunt talk she seemed to like us, and made more effort than anyone else to bridge the divide between our group's Old World old and New World young. She taught me the few lines of Provençal dialect I can still muster, including *Fa cao l'estiu*, which translates roughly as, 'She's hot out here, all right.'

On the stroke of noon we'd stop for lunch, about a dozen of us gathering around rough tables in cool stone huts. We usually brought our own food: baguettes filled with *saucisson*, the French salami, or camembert cheese. Occasionally, a crop of home-grown *pois chiches*, or chick-peas, would appear in a huge bowl on the table. We'd help ourselves, adding chopped onion, tomato, *cornichon* – pickled cucumber – and boiled egg. After a drenching in olive oil, it was ready to eat.

And we drank. How we drank. We glugged down the red wine made the year before with fruit drawn from the same vineyards in which we worked. It was a rough-and-ready blend of the workhorse grape varieties that clothe the southern French littoral – Grenache, Carignan, Cinsault, perhaps a bit of Syrah. It was light – usually only about 11 percent alcohol – simple, and improved by being slightly chilled. The hearty draughts we downed from Arcoroc tumblers barely touched the sides.

We drank for every possible reason: for refreshment; for taste – it was a dependable companion for the simple foods we ate; and for the effect the alcohol had on us. The wine took the edge off our soreness, raised our spirits and emboldened us for the long hot afternoons that lay ahead. It gave us energy. I used to marvel at the ferocity of my post-lunch attack on the vines. At the time I was ignorant of the process that occurs in the liver whereby alcohol is transformed into a fuel source that instantly enters the bloodstream, ready to be burned up.

We drank knowing the bottle on the table was bottomless. Wine seemed less precious than the water supply. Like bread, it was an essential daily nutrient, respected but seldom discussed. It was *vin*, a dull monosyllable with no chateau attached. There wasn't much else to it.

I have never again drunk wine the way I did during those weeks 26 years ago.

Cut to a cellarful of noise in Wellington, some two decades later. The Beaujolais Wine Bar is packed for one of its regular, rollicking tasting evenings. A tricolor hangs against one wall, and New Zealand's own peculiar blend of red, white and blue against another, illustrating the theme chosen by bar manager Andrew Parkinson: France v. New Zealand: a test match not of rugby, but of wine.

The wines are blind-tasted in a series of pairings, one-on-ones of the same grape variety and vintage. A Marlborough Sauvignon Blanc is tasted alongside a Pouilly Fumé from Sancerre, a Kumeu River Chardonnay against a white Burgundy, and so on. Andrew has done his best to match wines of comparable quality.

The usual happy, vociferous group of urbanites has gathered for the occasion. These people revel in wine. They love tasting it, enjoying it and talking about it. At each tasting they learn a little more, but they're there as much for the way wine connects them socially as for any other reason.

We taste each wine from an XL5, a small wine glass shaped like a closed tulip that was created to give the world a standard tasting glass. We jot down notes, mark each wine out of 20, and laugh as Andrew solemnly invokes rugby imagery. 'Getting ready for this first set piece ... a Marlborough méthode packing down against a big champagne house ... Engage!'

New Zealand, weighing in many dollars lighter, takes out a close contest. Not that it matters. The result is forgotten soon after the bottles are unmasked and people fill their glasses with their personal favourite (mine a 1997 fourth growth St Estèphe, a red Bordeaux) and talk the rest of the evening away.

These two vignettes from my career as a wine lover, juxtaposed like that, seem to me remarkable. They are separated by more than just half my adult life and two hemispheres: they are a revolution apart.

By 1979, the vintage I worked at Flayosc, the wine world had entered a restless period. Five years earlier the first Sauvignon Blanc vines had been planted in New Zealand, the genesis of a small but potent global force. By that time there were two wine worlds: Old and New, Europe and the rest. One was tired and inhibited by tradition; the other was innovative, flexible and hungry.

An innocent from a land of Cold Duck and Cresta Doré – and, of course, beer – I was ignorant of this changing tide. I felt I was immersing myself in timeless French *savoir vivre*. I was certainly being exposed to an ancient wine culture, but the surface reality was deceiving: I was in one of that culture's least valued and least refined corners, and an endangered one at that. French wine-drinking habits were shifting. Our cheap-litre-or-more-a-day labourer's habit was already becoming passé and so, as a consequence, were the wines we were helping to produce. Customs that had seemed solid and immutable were under threat.

Most of the vineyards in which we worked had been created about a century earlier to provide inexpensive sustenance and cheer to the grim lives of France's new industrial working class. Volume and value for money had dictated the recipe, and varieties like Carignan were good at that. The wine had been trundled north on the new railway system to be absorbed by the masses of *malheureux*, be they the factory fodder in Paris and the north-east, or the cannon fodder on the Western Front. It had not been uncommon for a working man to down six litres a day. During the Great War, Marie-Thérèse told me, the one-litre canteens of the French soldiers were filled regularly with cheap southern red. Desperate for more, the poor sods had the idea of enlarging these thin metal containers by soaking beans in them. When swollen, the beans would stretch the canteen, making room for another hopefully mind-numbing quarter of a litre or so.

Factory closure and unemployment spread like a plague through France in the second half of the twentieth century. The demise of the thirsty labouring class put the brakes on demand for cheap plonk. A burgeoning middle class of bank clerks, boutique owners, public servants and Renault reps had no desire to drown themselves in wine of marginal quality from filthy co-ops. They were attracted by good bottled wine in smaller quantities. Between 1980 and 1996, annual per capita wine consumption dropped from 91 litres to 60. In the 1950s it had been close to 135.

In 1979 the Flayosc co-op had no hope of selling all the wine it made. I can't say they couldn't give it away, because they did. We each received two litres a day on top of our wages, a concept we embraced with more ardour than was perhaps good for us. On some mornings we were a sorry-looking crew reporting for work. 'Infuse wild thyme and drink it,' Marie-Thérèse sternly instructed us, passing on an old Provençal cure for a hangover.

In those days the European Union was still buying the surplus wine, turning much of it into industrial alcohol and jettisoning the rest. The co-op was not accountable to the market. Its idea of a marketing plan was an opening hours sign tacked to the cellar door. Even so, helpless shrugs and dark prophecies about days of reckoning were not uncommon. Vine-pulling was starting to occur in the neighbouring Languedoc-Roussillon region.

A *co-vendangeur* and I were married at the end of our year in Provence. Marie-Thérèse presented us with

Flayoscais wine as a wedding present. We took some to London with us. I remember, months later, opening a bottle and sharing it with friends at a sunny afternoon picnic on Hampstead Heath. It was thin, harsh and basically awful. I struggled to understand how I could have drunk so much of it. Now I know that hard wines go best with hard lives.

We returned home in the early 1980s, to a country whose wine fortunes were moving in the opposite direction. After a century of promising starts but no innings of substance, New Zealand wine was finally taking off. The New Zealand Sauvignon Blanc revelation had made us a player in a changing global order.

The emergence of wine's New World had been led by California. A famous forerunner to my wine test match in Wellington had been a California v. France tasting contest held in Paris in 1976 with French judges. The Americans had put up their best cabernets and chardonnays. These had been blind-tasted with a number of Médoc *crus classés* and top white burgundies. For both reds and whites, the judges' overall favourites had been Californian. The rumblings of Gallic protest could not prevent the spread of the new truth: quality in wines was no longer the preserve of Europe.

During the 1980s California was joined by Australia, New Zealand, South Africa, Chile and Argentina, all of whose new wines delivered fresh bright intense fruit tastes at good prices. These wines – and their easily decipherable labels – fitted perfectly with the well-travelled younger generation in places such as London, Chicago, Sydney and Wellington.

It takes a lot to unnerve the great brands of Champagne, Bordeaux and Burgundy, and European Union subsidies continued to prop up bulk producers of the south, such as the *coopérative vinicole de Flayosc*. But 2003 produced a statistic that was impossible to ignore: that year more Australian wine than French was sold in the United Kingdom. The French had been knocked off a pedestal they had occupied for centuries.

The last time I went to Flayosc, several years ago, there were certainly fewer vineyards. EU persuasion had started to make inroads, and the moneyed middle class that had rejected the *vin ordinaire* of its forebears was now taking over the land on which it grew, to build their villas. But the co-op was still in business. Provence had been more fortunate than Languedoc-Roussillon: it had a marginally more elevated image, and Provençal rosé had become a popular brand. But the fundamental problems had not gone away. There is a growing wine surplus in the world, and it's all at the Flayosc end of the scale.

Marie-Thérèse had died. I imagine she went without much fuss, probably telling people she was looking forward to being finished with the whole business. I'm imagining her big, honest, weathered face now, as I tell her I'm writing a book called *How to Drink a Glass of Wine*. Her head rocks back and she laughs and laughs.

And Noah

began to be

a husbandman,

and he planted

Genesis 9:20 *a vineyard.*

Clinging vines

THE PLANT THAT gives us wine grapes belongs to the genus *Vitis*, a family of hardy, deciduous climbers from the northern hemisphere. Members of this far-flung clan — there are about 20 cousins in North America alone — all share surface similarities, but no others bear fruit to match the sweet juicy berries of the species *Vitis vinifera*.

Vitis vinifera's original home appears to have been the rugged temperate lands that stretch east from the land-locked Caspian Sea — territory that today falls within the borders of Armenia and Georgia. Several ancient collections of grape pips showing clear signs of cultivation have been found in Georgia. Carbon-dating has put their likely period of provenance at between 7000 and 5000 BC.

Both biblical myth and language support the region's claim. The book of Genesis pins world's first wine-maker status (along with first embarrassing drunken episode) on Noah, telling us the builder of the ark planted his vineyard soon after the floating zoo landed on Mount Ararat, Armenia's highest peak. And the word for wine in many of the world's languages (including our own) can arguably be traced back to the ancient Georgian noun *ghvino*.

Wine is, in essence, good *Vitis vinifera* juice allowed to turn bad. Sugar accounts for roughly a quarter of the content of a ripe grape, making the grape among the sweetest of fruits and an eager fermentation prospect. Fermentation is the process whereby sugar, with the helping hand of yeast, morphs into alcohol, releasing heat and carbon dioxide along the way. (If you're now expecting the relevant scientific equation, you've come to the wrong book.) Break the skin of any grape and fermentation will set in quickly and naturally, turning the juice from light and sweet to strong and sour.

It all sounds simple, and at its most basic level it is. The first wine ever to meet up with a human palate would probably have been liquid found sloshing around the bottom of a container that had been stacked so full of grapes some of the ground-floor fruit got squeezed.

We've managed to complicate the process spectacularly since then. But in doing so we've also spectacularly improved the quality of the finished product.

Wine production today is a game of two halves: viticulture, the growing of the grapes, and wine-making, which is what happens in the winery after the harvest. In the larger companies each of these areas is run by a specialist. In small operations the viticulturist and wine-maker are usually the same person.

Viticulturists dig holes deep into paddocks to find out what kind of soil they have below their feet. They peer into these holes, even disappear into them, and discuss them endlessly. They study temperature tables, rainfall tables and sunlight-hours tables. And that's just to select a suitable site.

From there the decisions come one after the other, beginning with the choice of vine variety and its most suitable representatives. In the business this is called clonal selection.

The viticulturists then decide how close together the vines should be planted, and which trellis system to use. They make calls on spraying, disease prevention, irrigation, managing the leaf canopy of the vines and, where necessary, crop-thinning – the sacrifice of potential fruit in order to raise the quality of what remains. On a grapevine, as in most horticulture, less means more.

As the fruit ripens, the viticulturists have to guard their crops against the ravages of birds. In New Zealand, where birds are particularly rapacious, twenty-first century scarecrows include shotguns, gas-powered cannons and, most commonly, netting. A grower I met in Gisborne has a cheaper method: he places rabbit carcasses around his vineyard. These attract the large carrion-loving hawks, whose presence in turn keeps away the starlings and blackbirds. Starlings are a particular menace: a single bird can demolish 60 to 80 grapes a day.

The irony is that nature's original motivation for creating the sweet dark fruit of the vine was probably to attract birds. Birds were the original spreaders of grape seeds and, as such, ensured the species' survival for millions of years.

And then of course there's the weather, which can swing with alarming ease between saviour and slayer. The sun is crucial for ripening – it was Galileo who described wine as 'sunshine held together by water'. Frost and rain at the wrong times can dish up the unplayable balls of viticulture.

Autumn is a decisive season in the vineyard. If the ripening process is derailed by a less than sunny summer, a golden autumn can put things back on track. New Zealand's reliably benign, clear-skied autumns play a big role in the success of the country's wines. They draw out the ripening time, making it ideal for nurturing and holding in aromas, flavours and acidity. Hotter climates will ripen grapes more quickly and easily, but the result is often bland wine with lower levels of acidity. If hot sun were all that was required to grow good wine grapes, countries such as Algeria would make the best wine on the planet.

An ideal autumn is also one that allows producers to pick their grapes at the moment of their choice. As harvest time approaches, eyes squint nervously skyward: a heavy downpour will split open ripe fruit and leave it susceptible to rot.

'Good wine is made in the vineyard' is the mantra you'll hear in any serious winery. Like an actor with a script, a wine-maker is given raw material from which to try and create something beautiful. The quality of the material is critical. If a good wine-maker is given great fruit, the wine almost makes itself. Like Laurence Olivier in *Hamlet*, the wine-maker will simply lay bare the truth. But when the fruit has suffered through poor weather, craft and skill really come into their own. A wine-maker's true competency is tested in a difficult vintage.

Today's wineries are wildernesses of stainless steel. Were it not for the all-pervading thick, yeasty odour of alcohol creation, they could be mistaken for dairy factories. In most cases the machine-crushed grape juice is poured into gleaming vats to ferment. With red wine, the grape skins (and sometimes the stems) are included to lend colour, extra flavour and tannins. When juice from red grapes is denied this contact with the skins, the result is rosé, or even white wine.

Tannins supply red wine with many of its extra dimensions. Astringent, bitter compounds, they are felt in the mouth, rather than tasted. They're responsible for those hard, drying, puckery sensations we often get from red wine. Tannins come in different shapes and sizes – you'll hear wine buffs talk about harsh tannins, gentle tannins, green tannins and ripe tannins. They are invisible – until they 'drop out' of the wine over time to become sediment.

There are a few farms left in Europe where grapes are still crushed using human feet. The practice went into decline when the labour supply began to dry up in the 1960s, although it is being revived in the making of port in Portugal's Douro Valley. Besides providing great theatre, human foot-stomping ensures grape pips are left intact. Crushed pips do not release a pleasant taste.

Extinction does not always come easily to the old unmechanised ways of wine production. Several years ago I was invited by Neil McCallum, proprietor of Dry River wines in Martinborough, to plunge into one of his vats of fermenting Pinot Noir. This was in the name of *pigeage*, as the French call it: the act of pushing down and breaking up the crust of skins and stems that forms at the top of a vat of fermenting red wine. The aim is to increase the contact between the juice and the solid material from which it extracts all that richness. Various modern instruments and gadgets have been created for the task, but McCallum is not alone in thinking nothing's quite as effective as the gentle, smooth limbs of a hominid, the method used by the twelfth-century Cistercian monks in Burgundy.

If the opportunity ever comes your way to be a *pigeagist* (if there is such a word), jump right in. It is a singularly strange sensation. A jam-like swamp envelops your legs with a heavy intimacy. It is pleasantly warm, up around 32°C. 'Ferment' essentially means 'boil', and you feel the energy and turbulence of the process as carbon-dioxide bubbles constantly break on the surface.

The carbon dioxide can be a problem: stories abound of cellar-hands in Burgundy collapsing from lack of oxygen and drowning in the rich soup. Neil McCallum's vat was virtually in the open air, which ensured my lungs were well-served. And if you're wondering about hygiene, rest assured that fermentation is a hostile environment for potential pathogens.

The wine my immersion helped create – the 1999 Dry River Pinot Noir – seems to me, whenever I have the chance to taste it, a fantastic advertisement for this ancient practice.

Usually fermentation continues until there's no sugar left. This takes roughly a week for most red wine, much longer for some whites. Sometimes the process shuts down when the yeast, stifled by the concentration of the alcohol, throws in the towel. On other occasions the wine-maker may call things off to retain some residual sugar, depending on the style of wine that he or she wants to produce. It's a common misconception that grape variety determines the level of sweetness in a wine. In reality any grape can be made into dry or sweet wine.

At this point, the wine is in the can, a raw cut in need of refinement. It tastes like – well, good grape juice turned bad. All the main components are there, but they are ungainly and at odds with each other. Settling them down, splicing them together and adding some special effects is the next step.

Wine-makers have a lot of options and techniques at their disposal, and the application of these varies greatly between wines of different colours and styles. Perhaps the most significant agent for change from here on is oak. Wine's relationship with the oak tree goes back nearly two millennia. The conquered Gauls began making containers using oak staves held together by iron hoops to ship their wine to Rome, which was becoming a thirsty city by the third century AD. The architecture of the oak barrel has barely changed since.

The essential tools in its construction have also remained the same: a pair of hands and a strong back. What has altered is its purpose. A barrel's value no longer derives from its ability to be easily rolled up and down the gangplank of a quinquereme, but mainly from the flavours and structure it can pass on to wine. For any red wine to be a serious cellaring prospect, time in an oak barrel is essential. Among whites, oak figures mostly in the making of Chardonnay, and occasionally in Pinot Gris and Sauvignon Blanc.

On the flavour side of things, oak sweetens a wine. Today the two primary sources of oak barrels are France and America. As you'd somehow expect, most American oak supplies more obvious, sweeter flavours (coconut and vanilla are prominent) than its French counterpart. This makes American oak a favourite among many Australian producers, who see it as a good match for their Shiraz and other powerful reds. The subtler spicy, cedary characters derived from French oak are key ingredients in serious Bordeaux blends and Burgundy.

What is extraordinary, on this deforested planet of ours, is that there are legions of century-old oak trees in France and the rest of Europe queuing up for a wine-barrel afterlife. France currently produces around 200,000 oak barrels annually and – due in part to inspired environmental policy dating back to the seventeenth century, when concern over the oak-hungry shipbuilding industry led to extensive government replanting pro-grammes – is quite relaxed about its ability to feed climbing global demand.

The French coopers are on to a good thing. The cost of a 228-litre Burgundian barrique to a New Zealand producer is between NZ$1200 and NZ$1400. The bar-rique will hold just 25 cases of wine and its useful life in the winery will be only about five years. The French are clawing back something from the upstart New World's success.

Tricky ways to slash the exotic timber bill include the use of oak chips, mainly employed by large-scale producers. Sacks of these chips, sarcastically dubbed 'micro-barriques' by small artisan producers, are left to soak like giant tea bags in tanks of fermenting juice. They succeed in imparting oak flavours but bring none of the other benefits of barrel maturation. In most parts of the world they're not illegal, but producers can be coy about admitting to using them. Inexpensive drink-now Chardonnays and Shirazes with a vague mention of 'oak maturation' on their labels are likely to have had a serving of chips on their way through.

There are some important finishing touches before bottling. Most have to do with removing solids (for example, dead yeast cells, grape skins and stems) and clarifying the wine to prevent cloudiness. I shared the horror of most wine drinkers when told, for the first time, about some of the traditional 'fining agents' used to soften and clarify wine. Egg whites and milk I could accept, but delights such as dried ox blood and fish bladders were another matter. However, only minute traces of these ever end up in the finished wine, and some of the agents are now either illegal or out of favour.

If several grape varieties or batches are destined for a wine, blending is also a necessary step. Many wine-makers will tell you how much they enjoy this part of the process. Suddenly they're no longer farmers or plant managers, but noses and mouths. By tasting and evaluating different combinations, they're able to dictate what the finished wine will be like. They finally get to wrest control from God.

The art of getting the most from wine is not complicated. But it does have to be learned.

Hugh Johnson

Learning to imbibe

THE MECHANICS OF drinking a glass of wine are good to know, in the same way that it's useful to know something about correct batting technique before you walk out on to the crease in a game of cricket. Your natural instincts, no matter how good they are, will be insufficient.

Before we begin, a minor digression on the verb 'to drink'. It is a typical Anglo-Saxon 'doing' word, an unpretentious, unmelodious jab. Drinking is undeniably what you do (or should do) with a glass of wine. But it's a word that lacks precision. A baby at the breast drinks. So does my car, a serious quaffer of 91 unleaded.

In both cases regular nourishment governs the agenda, and the intake is passively accepted.

At Flayosc, my friends and I 'drank' wine. From here on in this book, drinking a glass of wine becomes a more selective activity. It will be concentrated on the part of the drinking universe that involves tasting, exploring and – most important of all – enjoying. In fact I looked at using one of those three verbs in the title. I even considered 'consume', that favourite of many wine people. None of these alternatives, though, seemed able to fill the space as well as 'drink', with all its big, overflowing, Falstaffian connotations.

Our family has a favourite Mr Bean skit. Our socially clapped-out anti-hero is dining alone in a restaurant. Soon after admiring a birthday card he's written to himself, he orders wine. When the waiter offers him a taste he looks, sniffs – and before raising the glass to his lips – listens. Lips pursed, face idiotically quizzical, he swirls the wine beside one ear, then the other.

Whenever I taste a wine, whether at home or in a restaurant, my kids mimic Mr Bean, exaggeratedly giving their glasses the aural treatment. Their implication is that he may be a moron but he has a point: how many senses do we really need to call on – ostentatiously – to appreciate a glass of wine?

The answer is four: sight, smell, touch and taste. Any experimentation is to be commended though. Mr Bean may turn out to be ears ahead of his time.

Once your glass of wine has been poured – no more than half full, as you need plenty of room to poke your nose in – hold it away from you, against a white background if possible, and inspect its contents. There are several reasons for this visual once-over. The first is aesthetic. The colour of wine is endlessly varied, and beautiful in its own right. Photographers never seem to tire of the jewel-like quality of a glass of wine refracting light.

The wine's colour also offers hints as to its style and age. A lighter-bodied red will be more translucent than a blockbuster. Older red wines assume a brick-cum-orange tinge, noticeable around the wine's rim, while white wines deepen toward amber as they age.

Don't worry too much about the clarity. If your wine appears cloudy, it could be faulty, but the cause is more likely to be that the wine-maker decided not to filter it. Many New Zealand Pinot Noirs have a slightly cloudy aspect because their makers believe filtration denies them complexity.

Now give your glass a whirl. Hold it by the stem and rotate. (Mysteriously, men tend to rotate their wine glasses anti-clockwise, while women go for clockwise. Feel free to analyse that.) Like much to do with wine-tasting, swirling a glass can appear pretentious. And yet it's as practical an act as stirring a cup of tea. The main purpose is to release more of the wine's flavour compounds. You can also get an indication of the wine's alcoholic strength from the 'tears' that form on the inside of the glass. The more viscous, or sticky, the tears appear to be, the higher the wine's alcohol content.

Now it's time to get serious. Wine connoisseurs are sometimes called 'noses', after their single most important instrument. If you lose your sense of smell, you lose much of your ability to taste. (Just think back to the last ghastly head-cold you had.) This is because when you're tasting something in your mouth, you're still smelling it via the retro-nasal passage that connects the back of the mouth to the nose. Much of what we attribute to taste is really our sense of smell. There are taste buds on the tongue, but the information they process and send to the brain's olfactory bulb – Flavour Central – is limited in comparison to the work done by the thousand or so different receptors in the nostrils and the retro-nasal passage.

Taste and smell converge more in some foods than in others. For me, strong French goat's cheese epitomises this blurring of the boundary between the two senses. I'm somehow already biting into the cheese with my nostrils. Wine behaves in the same way.

'Bouquet' is not, as many people believe, the sum of smells you get from a particular glass of wine. Strictly speaking, it refers only to the smells acquired through the wine-making and ageing processes, while smells that spring from the fruit itself are called 'aromas'. The dividing line is a little messy, but as an example a three-month-old Sauvignon Blanc will exude aromas. With a six-year-old Cabernet Sauvignon it will be mainly bouquet.

Whether you're drinking socially or as part of a tasting group, you should always sniff a glass of wine before you drink it. Sniff and concentrate – partly for sensual entertainment, partly to find out things. A wine's smells are a window to its soul. The more times you make a conscious effort to sniff before drinking, the more you'll appreciate how complex and different wines can be. With the aid of informed fellow drinkers, you can also learn to translate the messages the nose is relaying and start to recognise individual smells.

These aren't all necessarily pleasurable. If a wine is suffering from cork taint – an ailment caused by mould growing on the cork – you'll get a whiff of dank pinex or cardboard. A corked wine diagnosis can be confirmed by turning your nostrils' attention to the cork itself. If it smells of cork rather than wine, your bottle is definitely suffering from cork taint. Of course, this has all been less of a problem since the screw-cap revolution.

A white wine that is oxidised – a fault caused by excessive exposure to oxygen when the wine was being made – will give off a stale, baked-apple odour. Herbal leafy smells are indicative of unripe grapes. Unripe New Zealand Cabernet Sauvignon can sometimes smell interestingly like cannabis.

It's unusual, but in these days of high-alcohol wines you can occasionally pick up a sweet, spirity odour. I once tasted, from a well-known producer in the Russian River region of California's Sonoma County, a Pinot Noir in which the fruit aromas were overwhelmed by boozy fumes. This is not good: it shows the wine is seriously out of balance and will be overly 'hot' in the mouth.

Wine-making techniques are also revealed through smells. The use of oak comes through via woody, spicy notes; secondary — or malolactic — fermentation results in buttery, milky scents.

Many grape varieties immediately declare their identity through their aromas. This is particularly true of that club of white wines known as 'aromatics', so-called because they exude powerful fruit perfumes that occur naturally, rather than as a result of anything the wine-maker has done. They and their signature aromas are: Gewürztraminer (spices, lychee), Sauvignon Blanc (cut grass, the infamous cat's pee, tropical fruit), Riesling (flowers, honey) and Pinot Gris (apples, pears, stone fruit). Among red wines, good quality Pinot Noir has the capacity to deliver a dazzling, highly evocative array of scents.

And so to your palate. Let the liquid wash over and around your tongue's taste buds like an incoming tide enveloping coastal boulders. Keep it in your mouth for a while, churning it around before swallowing. (We're drinking here, not spitting.)

Now stop everything and think. Conduct your internal enquiry. Did the taste confirm the findings of the nose? Or was there a further flavour surprise? Was the taste sweet, dry, or somewhere in-between? Was there a softness to the wine, or did it perhaps have a noticeable acidic backbone? Was its texture viscous or thin? What kind of presence did the tannins have? Was there heat, caused by excessive alcohol? Were all the elements in balance? After swallowing, did it leave you with a pleasant, lingering aftertaste, or did the wine's presence fall away abruptly?

And last but not least, did you like it?

My dear girl, there are some things that are just not done, such as drinking Dom Perignon '53 above the temperature of 38° Fahrenheit.

James Bond in *Goldfinger*

Pleasure

WHEN YOU SIT down to a glass of wine, you should heed Joel Grey's welcome to his audience at his louche little Berlin nightclub in *Cabaret*: 'Leave your troubles outside — because here life is beautiful.' A glass of wine is one of life's punctuation marks, a pleasurable pause. You will enjoy it more if you come to it already relaxed and emptied of care, rather than expecting it to achieve this happy state for you.

Nor should you let gravitas get the better of you, even if you're taking part in a structured tasting with multiple wines and all the trappings. There are few things more absurd than a silent, politburo-grim table of wine-tasters. Wine is a source of enjoyment and good health and should always be approached in that spirit, no matter what the occasion.

Wine is people. Even when performing a sacred duty in a church, it still acts as a bringer-together – 'communion' means as much. This is not to say it can't be a solitary pleasure: I seldom cook without a glass of wine at my elbow. It's just best enjoyed in the company of others.

The better the wine, the more important this becomes. The idea of someone on their own opening and drinking a bottle of truly great wine, say a 1945 Château Latour from Bordeaux, is almost too shocking to contemplate. Beauty is always amplified and more affecting when it is shared. And besides, where does drinking without company leave wine's tongue-loosening effect?

Many people would probably tell you the best bottle of wine they ever had was shared with only one other person. Wine has ever been the drink of lovers because of its light sensual qualities, because it goes so well with food and, of course, for the lift alcohol gives the libido. A bottle contains three drinks each for two people, a stimulating dosage. God knows how many of us were begat through the heady mix of Bacchus and Eros. A name that comes to mind is that of the tragic Hollywood starlet Margaux Hemingway. The granddaughter of Ernest

Hemingway was so named because she was conceived on the night her parents polished off a memorable bottle of Château Margaux.

You should always take your time over a glass of wine. Its complex flavours make it a drink to savour. Be wary of those who gulp wine as if it's water. Like those who bolt their food, there's a good chance they'll be lousy lovers: they want to satisfy the appetite too quickly.

Correct temperature is essential. The same bottle served at different temperatures will not give you the same tastes. In New Zealand we like our beer cold, and in many restaurants it often shares a fridge with the white wine. As a result, some quite complex whites come to the table gustatorily strait-jacketed.

The problem surrounding most reds is somewhat different. We are often told to serve red wine at room temperature, but what temperature is that? After my daughters have cranked up the central heating, my living room would be many degrees hotter than the French château in which the term *chambré* (meaning 'at room temperature') was first coined.

Lower temperatures dampen aroma and fruit flavours, and exaggerate tannins, bitterness and oak character. Higher temperatures soften tannins but exaggerate alcohol and sweetness. In sparkling wines, higher temperatures cause more carbon dioxide to be released via larger bubbles, making the wine too frothy. The heat also seems to flatten the acids.

With all that in mind, here are some general recommendations on serving temperatures:

Dense, complex reds	15°–18°C
Complex dry whites	12°–16°C
Light, refreshing reds (for example, Beaujolais)	10°–12°C
Sweet, sparkling and lower-quality red and white wines, and rosés	8°–10°C

My final word on temperature concerns microwaves. People have sworn to me that a quick zap in the microwave is the perfect way to raise the temperature of a bottle of red wine. I've tried it once and it certainly didn't spoil the wine, but every second it was in there I was terrified the bottle was going to explode. I'm old-fashioned. I also believe wine does not enjoy sudden shocks.

Having the right glass is also of prime importance, particularly if you're drinking really good wine. Those intricately cut jobs shaped liked upturned bells, which your mother was so pleased to find in a second-hand store, are, truth be known, good only for chocolate mousse. The essentials for any wine glass are that it be clean, reasonably big (to provide a roomy smelling chamber) and clear (in order for you to properly assess the wine's colour). It must have a stem (so you can hold the glass without affecting the temperature of the wine) and the top of the glass should turn inwards (to hold in as much of the aromas or bouquet as possible).

If you want to play it safe and not spend too much, the XL5 or standard international tasting glass is not a bad option, although it is too small for any special occasion.

At the other end of the scale are the expensive masterpieces of Riedel. This Austrian family has been making glassware (they call it 'stemware') for 250 years. Current head Georg Riedel has made a science out of creating wine glasses to suit specific wines, and travels the world promoting them. A serious man who looks and behaves uncannily like Captain von Trapp in *The Sound Of Music*, Reidel consults exhaustively with winemakers to determine which elements of a wine should be enhanced and which played down. He then sets out to design a glass that will ensure the wine's best side is put before your taste lens. For example, we register acidity on the edges of the tongue: Riedel's Sauvignon Blanc glasses therefore attempt to channel the wine away from that area, to minimise the effect of the acidity.

If, for whatever reason, you are obliged to drink poor wine, you can help disguise the wine's weaknesses by chilling it. You should also make sure you match it with very ordinary glassware. A Riedel would have had the many imperfections of my Flayosc wine hollering for attention.

Then there's food, which is central to the enjoyment of wine. Wine can seem to change when partnered with food, and vice versa. This is because the human palate is 'flavour-malleable': any distinctive taste has the effect of altering the perception of what comes next. If you take in salt water during a swim at the beach, the cold freshwater shower directly afterward will taste sweeter in your salty mouth than you ever thought possible. Wine and food couplings work in the same way. For instance, a sour acidic food such as a salad with vinegar dressing will lower your perception of sourness in an accompanying wine, making the wine seem mellower.

More has been written about the so-called best and worst wine and food couplings than the subject has ever merited. Really there are no rules. Ancient decrees such as 'white wine with white meat, red wine with red', or the French favourite 'red wine with cheese', are too imprecise and sweeping to be of any help.

Go exploring. In my opinion, the most versatile – and, some would argue, the best – food wines are light, well-balanced and acidic. Aromatic whites all fit that description, as does a lot of Pinot Noir.

Heavy, oaky, tannic Cabernet Merlots and Syrahs need to be accompanied by rich red meats and stews, certainly not everyday fare. Without *any* food, these wines can give you stomach churn. In many ways, they are themselves food. More than one Australian wine-maker has offered me his latest soupy, blockbuster Shiraz with the proud announcement, 'Steak and eggs in a glass, mate!'

Paralleling the recent rise of wine in New Zealand has been a rise of interest in Asian cuisine. More than half the restaurants in Wellington, where I live, are now Asian. The two developments are somewhat contradictory, as the taste and texture of wine is easily overwhelmed by a tongue-burning lamb korma or nasi goreng. When food has been prepared with dramatic doses of piquant spices, beer is usually the best beverage.

Finally, you should try and approach every glass of wine with a *tabula rasa*. Try to delete from your consciousness any information you may have received about the wine. Forget about any medals it may have won, scores it has been given by critics, opinions you may have heard. Above all, forget the price you paid for it.

Don't think of it as anything but a glass of wine. Drink, and let it reveal itself.

I can certainly see you know your wine. Most of the guests who stay here wouldn't know the difference between **Basil Fawlty,** *Fawlty Towers* *Bordeaux and claret.*

The peripatetic palate

EVERY TIME YOU drink a glass of wine, you bring with you every previous glass of wine you've ever tasted. The sum of these encounters forms the basis of your palate knowledge. The more you get out, in the wine sense, trying new and different wines, appraising them and learning something about them, the deeper and more acute this knowledge will be.

At the Ivy League end of the scale are the rigours of the Master of Wine course. This is a serious investment both in time and money, and one usually made for career reasons. At the other extreme is Friday night drinks at the office, wheeling in different wines each week and swapping opinions on them between the shop-talk and gossip.

Developing palate knowledge is akin to becoming well-read. With books you begin young – curling up, perhaps, with *Peter Pan*. The pleasure of it takes you by surprise. You tell people of your excitement. They recommend other books. You become a reader.

Reading well is not about reading vast amounts at speed. It's about being receptive to the magic and meaning of a good book, and about exposing yourself to many different kinds of books so you learn to distinguish between, say, serious novels and light holiday reads. The first serious novels you devour in your teens leave impressions that are never lost. Holden Caulfield, Jay Gatsby and Connie Chatterley are still with me, as clear as the day several decades ago I first met them on the page. That's because they stepped out on to a blank slate, awakening new senses.

I formed similar attachments with the first wines of any profundity I tasted.

After many years of wine-drinking, you will be less easily impressed. You will also have tasted so many wines it will be difficult to remember many of them. A wine, like a book, has to be very good now for me to remember it in any detail, unaided, a few years later. (Age and degeneration may have come into play as well.)

Not everybody is so challenged. One of the most

extraordinary things I've read about American taster Robert Parker concerns his palate memory. He has tasted 10,000 wines a year for the past 30 years and can apparently recall the tastes and smells of every one.

Recording impressions in a tasting diary helps cover for a porous memory. It's a must if you're tasting a few wines a week and want to get the most from your expanding knowledge. Having to verbalise your impressions also helps you focus more on the act of tasting.

What also happens over time is that the more you know, the less sure you can become. Through breadth of exposure, I'm more aware of nuance and possibilities than I was some years ago. As a result, I'm also less forthright in my opinions, especially at blind tastings. I've been exposed to too many Pinots that behave like Syrahs, and too many unwooded Chardonnays that taste very like Sauvignon Blancs, to be sure of anything. The celebrated English wine merchant Harry Waugh, when asked whether he had ever mistaken a glass of Burgundy (Pinot Noir) for Bordeaux (predominantly either Cabernet Sauvignon or Merlot), memorably replied, 'Not since lunch.'

Unlike a favourite book, a bottle of wine can't be dusted off and enjoyed again. That's one of wine's paradoxes: the carefully constructed beauty and elegance we admire so much, we also destroy. The moment the wine slides below the oesophagus, our cranking digestive system begins its work, eventually reducing the glorious substance to something vile. A glass of wine is a one-off performance, a few fleeting moments when a combination of scents and tastes and textures briefly transports us somewhere else, the way good art should. And then it is gone forever.

My own wine history was not launched by a single, shining moment but one of suffering. It was 1960 and I was four. My family was living in London that year, and for a couple of summer weeks had rented a white villa with green shutters on the Île de Ré near La Rochelle. The fawn-coloured sands, Atlantic horizons and battalions of *colonies de vacances* children who daily invaded the beach were grainily immortalised on my father's 8-millimetre camera. He also showed a fondness for oxcarts, and coy Françoise Sagan look-alikes, brazenly shot at close range.

I must have worked up a healthy thirst on the beach this particular morning, as there I was, standing alone on the cool tiles of the villa kitchen, reaching for a bottle of grenadine, that lovely French cordial made from pomegranates. Or so I thought. The grenadine label, an elaborate circus-poster pastiche of flags and medallions, bore a strong resemblance to the one on the Martini bottle. I unwittingly poured myself a stiff Martini and took a greedy slug. It was the kind of loss-of-innocence king-hit your taste buds never forget.

When I was growing up there was always wine around – unusual in 1960s New Zealand. Most evenings my parents would share a bottle of McWilliams Bakano or Cresta Doré, or something from Montana. In the kitchen I would watch, fascinated, as my mother poured red wine into the frying pan she'd just used to grill steaks, scraped and swirled the contents around, and poured it all over the meat.

In a cupboard in his downstairs study, my father kept a cache of good stuff. At one time this was mostly French. In my early teens I would visit the cupboard just to admire the elegance of the label design and typography, along with the words themselves – Ch. Drapier & Fils, Entre Deux Mers, Chateauneuf-du-Pape. These bottles offered tangible proof that I wasn't too late: Old Europe was still alive, waiting for me to glide in and charm its *comtessas* at picnics in forests of oak and linden. At one point I amassed the empty bottles in my room. As the collection grew to resemble an occupying army, so did my mother's insistence that I collect only the labels.

By the time I was 17, my parents had discovered Australian red. I came to share this enthusiasm. By now I was not only stealing moments to admire the bottles, but also stealing the full bottles themselves. Seppelts Moyston Claret and Chalambar Burgundy were the first wines that astonished me in a positive way. They were dark, rich and velvety, worlds away from the thin, astringent New Zealand Bakano.

In the mid '70s, my palate development was temporarily arrested when I spent two years on a college basketball scholarship in a small town in Montana, USA. Being a student-athlete and Montana being a state of cowboys and pickup trucks, I drank mostly beer. When wine emerged — at a formal college 'Homecoming' dinner or some other similar occasion — it was usually pink and sweet and always had 'Ernest & Julio Gallo' on the label. I've avoided Gallo ever since — perhaps unfairly since the company has begun to produce some splendid wine. Nevertheless, it remains today what it already was back then — a vast California machine, the largest single wine-making establishment in the world. A year or so ago, one of the Gallo empire's tentacles reached out to New Zealand and wrapped itself around Marlborough's Whitehaven winery. As the wine world grows, it simultaneously seems somehow to contract.

When I moved there from America, France provided a great awakening. I was mesmerised daily by the array of wine on the supermarket shelves. My finances confined research to the lower end of the market, but my interest and appetite were both keen. Reluctant to restrict myself to the produce of the local *cave coopérative*, I explored whenever I could: bottles of dry bony Muscadet from the Loire in plastic-wrapped six-packs; lusher white Vouvrays, also from the Loire; Alsatian Rieslings; steely rosés from Tavel and other parts of Provence, and the plumper, fruitier ones from Anjou.

The reds I could afford included lower tier Côtes du Rhône and the wines of the southwest — Côtes du

Roussillon, Corbières, Minervois. I came to enjoy the austere gooseberry flavours of young Bordeaux, and learned to shop around and tune into wine conversations to discover which lesser-known châteaux were making good wine. In a wine-conscious land, you had to be quick. A good, sharply priced wine could vanish from a super-market shelf in a morning.

Occasionally I would splash out on a Burgundy, but the investment was never enough to cross that region's elevated quality threshold. I usually finished the bottle bitterly disappointed.

Some French friends were instrumental in my education. When I lived in Perpignan, Jacques Briu, who worked for a local wine company, Vignerons Catalans, would point me in the direction of the best small wineries in the *département*. Jacques is a proud Catalan who would, if he could, spend most of his time roaming the western Pyrenees hunting for boar, truffles, *cèpes* (wild mushrooms) and other mountain delights, none of which seem to have a hiding place he doesn't know about. I was given my first taste, in an omelette, of wild truffle by Jacques and his wife Suzette, who taught English with my partner.

In Provence, François and Maïcha Goy took us in like family. Maïcha made the wedding cake for our Flayosc nuptials, an amazing tower of almond and chocolate, and François introduced me to a variety of wines, among them the refreshingly light, sparkling

Clairette de Die, a product of the Drôme where he grew up. Eager to return François's magnanimity, I imported a bottle of inexpensive, late 1970s Hawke's Bay Cabernet. It was embarrassingly weedy and harsh, but François was gracious, comparing it to the strong Gris de Toul, a type of rosé made near the town of Toul in Lorraine. Was this, he wondered, the style the Hawke's Bay producers were aiming for? I couldn't bring myself to say that it was a New Zealand take on a Bordeaux red.

Just as French children at first seem clever to us because they speak such good French, it's easy to presume every Frenchman is a wine expert. The illusion is strengthened by the French fondness for not letting an under-supply of facts get in the way of a spirited discussion. I learned a lot about wine during those years, not least that it can be a favourite conversation topic for the garrulous and opinionated.

It was after leaving France that I got acquainted with a better class of French wine. This is not as anomalous as it seems: it is indicative of London's importance as a centre of the international wine trade. Living in the city briefly before heading back to New Zealand, I was given a job humping kegs and cases of wine at Arbuckle & Son, a disorganised liquor merchant near London Bridge. Arbuckle's wine warehouse was littered with the wreckage of carelessly (or perhaps not so carelessly) dropped cases of wine. My foreman, a red-headed Aussie called

Phil, invited me to help myself to any bottle that had survived these traumas.

Every night I was taking home wines bearing names such as St Estèphe, St Emilion, Nuits St Georges and Gevrey-Chambertin. I soon discovered that some pretty ordinary wine could be marketed under great names, and became more choosy. I learned to look for labels that also carried the name of an estate or vineyard. Unlike Basil Fawlty, I also learned that claret was wine from Bordeaux.

I finished at Arbuckle's a few days before Christmas. As a farewell gesture Phil loaded me up with the best bottles he could find. I thanked him and set out on the long walk to the tube station. I was weighed down like a packhorse. In my arms I held a mixed dozen, my shoulder-bag was full of bottles, and so were the deep side-pockets of my coat. My 'goodbye to London' shout for friends was looking promising, I mused.

But I'd been too greedy. Halfway across London Bridge, with night drawing in and snow starting to fall, I began to falter. I realised I had no show of getting it all back to home base in Shepherd's Bush. One of London's homeless was huddling against the side-rail of the bridge. I began handing him bottles – a second-growth Bordeaux, a Mosel Riesling, a Champagne. As each disappeared under his coat, the man's look of incredulity grew. 'Merry Christmas,' I said before moving on, feeling lighter and a little happier. I like to think he felt the same way.

Wine improves

with age.

The older I

get, the better

Anonymous *I like it.*

A good year

QUESTION: HOW DO you drink a glass of wine that is 420 years old?

Answer: With reverence, of course. And fast.

British wine writer Hugh Johnson was part of a small group which gathered in London in 1961 to taste what is believed to be the oldest bottle of wine to offer a pleasurable drinking experience. The wine was from Germany, specifically from the famous Stein vineyard on the steep sun-drenched slope that rises like an oversized rampart above the river Main and the city of Würzburg, the baroque capital of Franconia. It was probably made from the Sylvaner grape, a white variety that remains Franconia's staple and still covers most of the Stein vineyard.

Plenty of written evidence had been passed down about 1540, the wine's vintage year. Germany fried that summer. Apparently the Rhine was so dry you could stroll across it. In accordance with tradition, a huge commemorative cask was made to house the best of the vintage. It is an impressive sight, still squatting after all these centuries in the cellars of the Prince-Bishop's palace in Würzburg, its carved dial telling the tale of the wonderful wine that flowed in abundance that year.

In London, many empires and discovered continents later, the wine was uncorked and poured. 'The Stein-wein of 1540 was still alive,' Hugh Johnson later wrote in his book *The Story of Wine*. 'Nothing has ever demonstrated to me so clearly that wine is indeed a living organism, and that the brown, Madeira-like fluid still held the active principles of the life that had been conceived in it by the sun of that distant summer. It even hinted, though it is hard to say how, of its German origins. For perhaps two mouthfuls we sipped a substance that had lived for over four centuries, before the exposure to air killed it. It gave up the ghost and became vinegar in our glasses.'

We are hemmed in today by common miracles: tech-nological ones such as cellphones; natural ones such as bees making honey. Yet few are as fascinating as the mysterious capacity of some wine to endure and evolve into something deeper and more harmonious over time. I should emphasise the 'some'. Only a small, select club of wines has the potential to age well. About 80 percent of all wine bought in New Zealand – and probably everywhere else in the world – is opened within two hours of being purchased. It follows that the vast majority of wine is made for immediate consumption. And yet interest in ageing wine is certainly not dying. There appears to be an increasing number of private wine cellars, and certainly no shortage of small wineries serious about making what the French call *vins de garde*.

There is an element of protest in the way a vintage wine nails down a year, preserving a window into it for years to come. It is the sort of defiant little arm-wrestle with time that seems to preoccupy adults. Perhaps we are forever trying to recreate the comforting illusion of permanence we enjoyed as children, before we grew up and realised that most things and all people don't last, that the world is always tipping this way and that, and ultimately sliding out from under us.

I know of people who have bought a case or two of robust, built-to-last Hawke's Bay Bordeaux blends or Syrahs the year a grandchild is born. If the vintage is very good and the wine well-made and well-cellared, it might just make it through to be a talking point at the child's 21st birthday.

An experience I had in Australia recently suggested, however, that there's no guarantee how the birthday person will react. I was one of a group of journalists who were guests at the Brown Brothers winery in Milawa, north-east Victoria. Brown Brothers has a rich history. The original brothers started producing wine in the region when the Kelly Gang was in the saddle. Glenrowan, scene of Ned Kelly's famous final showdown, is just a few kilometres away.

Ross Brown, the charming chief executive, hosted an evening meal. Towards the end of the main course he decanted and poured a mystery wine, inviting us to identify it. It was red and old — that much was obvious. Someone got the grape variety right — Shiraz — but no one came close to picking the vintage, which was 1967.

The empty bottle was brought out to the table. Rising above the complimentary chatter about the nearly 40-year-old Shiraz, which was still drinking remarkably well, came a plaintive cry from one end of the table. John, a writer for an airline magazine, let it be known that he was born in 1967. He found drinking a wine that had lived a life in parallel with his own to be 'freaky' and 'not a pleasant experience', although he had difficulty explaining why. He kept shaking his head and muttering whenever he glanced at the label.

There's a lot we don't know about how wine matures. We can be sure that oxygen plays no part in improving wine over the long term. In fact, oxidation is probably the leading cause of death of bottled wine. The positive developments that occur inside a carefully cellared bottle result from reactions described as 'reductive'. An example of a reductive reaction is when the small astringent tannins in a young red wine coalesce into larger structures, resulting in a softer, less bitter wine.

The effects of time on colour and flavour are immediately obvious. A newborn red wine's intense garnet-purple will turn brick red-brown with age, and its vigorous flamboyant flavours will settle down. White wine will also deepen in colour toward amber, although over time flavours in white wines become bigger and more intense.

A wine's structure plays a major role in determining how long the wine will last before decline sets in. A wine that is well past its best is often described as having 'fallen apart'. The fruit presence collapses and the wine often becomes overly acidic. Red wines, which have a more complex structure than whites (mainly due to the presence of tannins), are generally better suited for cellaring, although some white wines such as Riesling, Chenin Blanc (Vouvray) and the great dessert wines also age well.

Ripe weighty fruit, an abundance of tannins and good acidity are all necessary if a red wine is to have ageing potential. High acidity is also one of the keys to longevity in whites, and always given as the reason Rheingau Riesling and French Vouvray age so beautifully.

Barrel-ageing also helps create wine that will keep, as does a long, slow fermentation process for reds.

There's a ready supply of tip sheets and expert predictions on the life spans of wines. The truth is no one really knows. The person in the best position to supply advice is always the wine-maker, whose knowledge of a wine is more intimate than anyone else's.

Old and great wines are unforgettable. They make lasting palate imprints; it's as if your taste buds can't bear to let them go. I have only tasted a handful that could be described as old and great, but these are wines that continue to haunt me.

Two stand out. The first was a 1945 Taylor's vintage port, which I tasted at the Beaujolais Wine Bar in Wellington in 1999. The year that saw off World War II was one of the century's great vintages, for port as well for Bordeaux. 'The 1945 Taylor's had a nose like a great claret,' I raved in my notes. 'Broad, gentle, slightly oaky. Nothing cloying – just rich concentrated cabernet-like depth. In the mouth it was heaven. The best kind of big. Not showy, just a lovely layered legato of vanilla and fine fruit.'

The other was a red Burgundy, a 1979 Louis Jadot Le Musigny, tasted in 2003 at the Maison Jadot winery in Beaune, where my host was the charming, irrepressible Jacques Lardière, Jadot's chief wine-maker. Never had I tasted a Pinot Noir so old (pinot vines being virtually non-existent in New Zealand in 1979), nor one from such hallowed ground. Le Musigny is one of a royal circle of Burgundian vineyards that includes Chambertin, La Tâche and Romanée-Conti. These small parcels of land – the Musigny vineyard is only 10.8 hectares in size and Jadot owns but a sliver of it – produce wines widely regarded as Burgundy's finest.

The bottle we had at lunch that day would have been worth well over $10,000. After 24 years in the bottle, it still had an extraordinarily vibrant core of sweet fruit, which seemed to shine softly, like a pearl. Around it hung warm, silky-smooth tannins and delicate spice flavours. The texture was supple, the weight perfect.

At the heart of both these wines was a sweet, seamless stillness.

Good cellaring conditions – especially low, constant temperature – are essential for wines to develop to such perfection. My own cellar is shamefully inadequate, and I keep delaying the tunnelling project that would improve it. Perhaps I'm suspicious of the rotten rock on which my house – and much of Wellington – is built. Or perhaps I'm held back by the sad memory of the first wine cellar with which I had a close association.

It was 1968, and the previous year's Montana Pinotage was being heralded as something special. My father, ever fond of characterful red, liked it enough to buy six cases from the little wine shop on Spa Road in Taupo. Never before had he tried to cellar anything seriously and I think he thought our bach at the lake would be a good place to start. Not being there most of the year would go some way towards removing the temptation to quaff the wine early.

The Pinotage was duly secreted in a downstairs cupboard, which was in a dark corner close by an earth bank. I watched attentively as my father screwed a bolt on to the creosoted door, then added a padlock. This was our version of Tutankhamen's tomb.

When, I enquired, would we start enjoying this treasure? 'Perhaps at your sister's wedding,' he replied with a grin. I began calculating. Kerry was 17. If she were to marry at 25, which seemed a good age to get married, that would take us to 1976. Eight years – more than half my life to that point – seemed an eternity.

The following year my father did something he'd never done before: he let the bach over the winter. Some young working men came for a look and enthused over its 1920s' charm. A deal was struck. They would rent the upper storey. The lower bedroom would be out of bounds. My father decided to leave the wine, thinking it would be safe behind the second padlock he put on the bedroom door.

Disquiet set in when midway through that year a friend of my sister said she'd been at a great party at our Taupo place the previous weekend. Similar reports followed. It turned out the young men were socially very active. They had installed coloured lights along the driveway and flung wide the doors almost every night.

The following summer I was with my father when he entered the downstairs bedroom. The door had been forced. So had the cupboard door. Our cellar was empty. Seventy-two bottles of 1967 Montana Pinotage had vanished down the throats of Taupo's young and restless. My father was crestfallen but stoic. After a few comments about how weak and untrustworthy people could be, he set off for a game of tennis.

Wine ... offers a greater range for enjoyment and appreciation than possibly any other purely sensory thing which may be purchased.

Ernest Hemingway

Adaptation

NO TWO GLASSES of wine are exactly the same – even when they're drawn from the same bottle. The first glass of a young bottle of wine, for example, will often have a tight, closed quality.

And a glass of wine, left to sit quietly between sips, will change. As time passes, the flavours broaden. The differences are due to wine's volatile relationship with oxygen, but they also reflect its chameleon-like nature. Variation is a big part of what wine is about.

This variation cuts many ways. There are obvious divisions such as red and white, and still and sparkling.

Beneath these are endless subdivisions. No vintage is the same as the last. Each patch of earth, with its own climate, will lend distinctive qualities to a wine. Each cellar has its own characteristics, so that two identical bottles emerging from hibernation in different cellars may not taste like close kinfolk at all. On top of this, every wine-maker has and applies a different philosophy and techniques. All this variability prompted the great writer and wine merchant André Simon to remark, 'There are no great wines – only great bottles.'

The sum of all the environmental factors that play a role in producing wine is encapsulated in the French word *terroir*. *Terroir* is an interesting concept. The French have proclaimed it loudly in recent years, in part because its central premise – that a wine's character directly reflects its place of upbringing – confirms their wines' uniqueness. And *terroir* works on both macro and micro levels: not only is the wine of Burgundy inimitable, so is the personality of every vineyard inside Burgundy.

But cosy and romantic as it would be to think that every glass of wine you drink connects you to a distinct plot of vines, for most of the wine consumed today it just isn't so. The large Australian companies have a 'to hell with *terroir*' attitude. Jacob's Creek, Yellowtail and the other monster brands are made by lumping together grapes grown all over Australia. The same is true of most of the less expensive wines everywhere, including those from New Zealand. For a wine that expresses a particular site you have to seek out what is called a 'single vineyard' wine. More of these are emerging as the New World's understanding of its vineyards and wine styles evolves, but *terroir* is always something for which you pay a bit extra.

Finally, there is the variety of the varieties. At last count an extraordinary 10,000 different vine varieties had been identified around the world, each one with its own flavour fingerprint. I've tasted around 120. That doesn't leave me with 9,880 still to find before I die, because the varieties currently being made into wine would number only between 1,000 and 1,500. French authorities have named just over 200 varieties of commercial significance in modern France.

Vitis vinifera ended up being such a fractured, multi-faceted species through its powers of adaptation. Whatever new environment it found itself in, it made itself comfortable by genetically mutating into a new variety. This chaotic urge to, as it were, turn over a new leaf is particularly marked in some vine varieties, and can occur almost instantaneously. Growers of the red grape Pinot Noir have become accustomed to some of their vines suddenly throwing out branches bearing white Pinot Gris fruit. Pinot Gris has close genetic connections to Pinot Noir.

Until recently, to trace the origins of vine varieties we relied on the odd written fragment and well-worn tales of doubtful authenticity. DNA testing has changed all that, and punctured several parentage theories. Shiraz, for instance, was for a long time believed to have come from Persia, where there is a city of the same name. One theory had it being transported to the Rhône Valley by Phoenician traders, another by returning Crusaders. Now a team at the University of California at Davis has established that Shiraz (or Syrah as it's known in France) has two parent vines, both French rather than Middle Eastern. One is the Mondeuse Blanche grape from the alpine Savoie region. The other is Dureza, a traditional red grape from the Ardèche.

Before the 2002 New Zealand general election, I wrote a column matching the party leaders to different varietal wines. (A varietal, by the way, is a wine named after that wine's dominant vine variety, with the necessary degree of dominance varying from country to country. So although there's a close link between varietal and vine variety, they are not the same thing.)

Labour prime minister Helen Clark was, I said, 'A Marlborough Sauvignon Blanc – clinically tank-fermented, piercingly acidic, more sour gooseberry than passion-fruit, the national flag carrier and much appreciated offshore.' Meanwhile, New Zealand First's Winston Peters was 'a Chardonnay, grown anywhere, pumped up with oak and a high alcohol content to suit popular tastes. The result is seductive, but offers only a veneer of complexity.'

So it went on. It was very easy to write because each grape variety has its own strong personality and is thus, like a politician, easy to caricature. When you sniff a wine and the grape variety's identity fair jumps out of the glass, the wine displays what is called 'good varietal definition' or 'good varietal signature'. In New Zealand, these individual signatures are particularly pronounced.

Given the remarkable diversity of vine varieties, most wine drinkers – and producers – confine themselves to an unadventurously small range. The usual suspects, which are known as the 'international varieties', come mostly from France, the country regarded for centuries as a kind of global wine HQ. The two leaders are Cabernet Sauvignon (red) and Chardonnay (white). From there the list includes the reds: Merlot, Pinot Noir, Syrah (Shiraz), Cabernet Franc and Sangiovese; and the whites: Sauvignon Blanc, Riesling, Gewürztraminer, Pinot Gris, Viognier, Muscat and Sémillon. These varieties have become the standards not just in the New World, but in many Old World countries that strive to stay apace with the demands of the international market. Bulgaria, for example, is now the world's second largest producer of Cabernet Sauvignon.

But although the international varieties may lead in ubiquity, they don't lead in volume. If you're ever looking for a good trivia question, here's one: What is the world's most widely planted grape variety? The answer is Airén, which occupies more than 400,000 hectares in

Spain. The reason you've never heard of it is because most of the fruit disappears into distilleries. Osborne brandy, whose forbidding silhouetted bull looms above Spanish highways, is largely the product of Airén.

For many years, New Zealand wine-makers were loathe to look beyond a small handful of tried-and-true international grape varieties. Recently, though, the field has broadened. Wines are now being made from such varieties as Roussane, Tempranillo, Montepulciano and Verdelho – although it has to be said that for obscurity none of these match Rkatsiteli and Saperavi, both of which are planted in Australia.

It gets even more interesting in the Old World. All over Europe, skirmishes are being fought to save regional varieties from oblivion. In Hungary there has been many an alarum about the decreasing presence of Kadarka in Bull's Blood, the country's renowned blended wine. Kadarka is Hungary's best-known indigenous red grape variety. Its powerful tannic presence provided Bull's Blood with its backbone, until it began to be displaced by the more easily-cultivated Kékfrankos from Austria and – horror of horrors – the more easily swallowed Merlot.

In northern Spain, Miguel Torres' vast wine empire is ticking along so nicely he can turn his attention to his personal passion: producing wines from the old and largely-forgotten Catalan varieties Samso and Garro. In Bulgaria, Mavrud and Melnik are on the comeback trail after years of relative neglect. Meanwhile, in Greece and Crete a new generation of young wine-makers has embraced hometown heroes such as the red grape Aigortiko and the aromatic white Malagousia. All these wine producers are trying to save part of their heritage, just as New Zealand Maori, Australian Aborigines, the Welsh and other colonised minorities have breathed life back into their ancient languages.

In New Zealand we don't have an indigenous grape variety, but in a few hundred years that may have changed. In my crystal ball I see a feral vine found in the foothills of the Kaikoura mountains. DNA testing shows it to be closely related to Sauvignon Blanc, but it has mutated into something quite strange. It will become known for a pronounced manuka character...

Wine makes a

man more pleased

with himself;

I do not say it

makes him more

Samuel Johnson *pleasing to others.*

To attain
paradise

OVER A CUP OF TEA, under a hairnet and behind her venetian blinds, my great-aunt would describe a couple living at the end of her street thus: 'They drink'. Her meaning was understood by all adults present. It wasn't just that the couple liked a tipple. The simple verb that sits at the heart of this book's title had been laden with judgement. My great-aunt's neighbours were, in her eyes, guilty of every imaginable irresponsibility and loose moral.

Another snapshot from the same file: As a child walking home from piano lessons along Tinakori Road, I slow to a dawdle in front of the Western Park Hotel to catch a glimpse of the public bar as silent patrons hurry in and out of the front door. I am rewarded with freeze-frames of a secret world where men stand drinking in their hats and overcoats, macerating in smoke and the reek of beer.

These scenes were part of a national confusion about alcohol when I was growing up. The Royal New Zealand Navy was the last navy in the world to continue giving its sailors a daily tot of rum. And yet New Zealanders also voted on local continuance or prohibition at every general election until 1990. New Zealand was often seen with a glass in its hand, but couldn't seem to get the guilty smirk off its face, or look very stylish doing it.

Drink, drank, drunk. If one glass keeps following another indiscriminately, you'll get hammered, or legless, or whichever of the hundreds of expressions for being drunk you feel like using, because wine is a powerful drug.

We wine writers seldom refer to wine's intoxicating effect, or the fact that most people drink wine to get drunk – maybe not howling-at-the-moon drunk, but at least a little happy. Yet we all know that this intoxicating effect is, and always has been, at the heart of the drink's allure. The human compulsion to seek temporary abandonment through whatever drug is handy is as ancient as it is irrational.

Such behaviour, according to New York gourmand and writer A.J. Liebling, is a necessary adjunct to life.

'No sane man can afford to dispense with debilitating pleasures; no ascetic can be considered reliably sane,' he wrote in his book *Between Meals*. 'Hitler was the archetype of the abstemious man. When the other krauts saw him drink water in the Beer Hall they should have known he was not to be trusted.'

I have sometimes mused that the job of a wine writer would be easier if wine were alcohol-free. I would be able to taste more wines, and in larger amounts, for one thing. For another, there wouldn't be the sly looks and the inevitable 'need-any-help-with-your-research?' comments. And all my fine words about aromatics, fruit expression and regional nuances would move from what some regard as a loony sideshow to centre stage. For wine would be about tasting pleasure and nothing else.

But then, of course, it wouldn't be wine. Alcohol, although invisible and essentially tasteless, is a mainstay which helps bind wine's other elements together. All that can change is the degree to which it is present.

Alcohol content generally ranges from 8 to 15 percent, although most of today's wines are at the upper end of the scale. This is particularly true of New Zealand wines. The country's high sunlight UV rating results in high levels of grape sugar, which in turn makes for high alcohol levels. Wine producers will also tell you high alcohol is what consumers want, and this is certainly true for some segments of the market. But the producers are also well aware that alcohol ratchets up a wine's volume in the mouth, making it more noticeable to a competition judge who is tasting hundreds of wines.

The form of alcohol in wine – which results from the fermentation process – is ethanol. Indeed ethanol is the alcohol in all alcoholic drinks. We perceive it as a faint, sweet and vaguely medicinal presence. Once ethanol enters the bloodstream, it goes to work supressing the central nervous system, with results most of us know well: a sense of well-being, unshackling of inhibitions, mild sedation, and the blunting of sensations such as pain. (While we're at it, let's add heightened libido.)

Excessive amounts change the picture dramatically. Lethargy, loss of coordination and nausea can take over, followed by bad sleep and a hangover. The long-term effects of heavy drinking are far more severe, and not confined to liver and brain damage. Alcohol abuse also contributes to many cancers, nerve- and muscle-wasting, blood disorders, accidental injuries and infertility.

Ancient civilisations showed varying attitudes to over-indulgence in wine. The Egyptians, for instance, didn't seem to consider intoxication a bad look at all. Wine was the drink of the Pharaohs and the elite. Tomb paintings of feasts show riotous behaviour, and the occasional person being sick. A woman in the Seventeenth Dynasty was recorded as saying, 'Give me 18 cups of wine, behold I should love drunkenness.'

In Greece, wine was revered and mostly treated with respect as an inebriant. Plato had hard and fast rules, declaring that boys under 18 should not drink at all (no mention of where that left the girls) and that moderation should be exercised until the age of 30. Among those not so cautious were followers of the cult of Dionysus, god of wine, who were usually hell-bent on achieving a state of drunken frenzy.

Around 375 BC the Athenian poet and playwright Eubulus offered some advice on how much was too much: 'Three bowls do I mix for the temperate: one to health, which they empty first, the second to love and pleasure, the third to sleep. When this bowl is drunk up, wise guests go home. The fourth bowl is ours no longer, but belongs to violence; the fifth to uproar, the sixth to drunken revel, the seventh to black eyes, the eighth is the policeman's, the ninth belongs to biliousness, and the tenth to madness and the hurling of furniture.'

If a Greek bowl was the equivalent of two modern standard drinks, which seems a reasonable assumption, New Zealand's Alcohol Advisory Council more or less concurs with Eubulus's prescription. These days though, the council also likes to stress the gender gap in alcohol tolerance. In any one week, it advises, men should drink no more than 21 standard drinks, and women no more than 14. There are seven standard drinks in a 750-millilitre bottle of wine, so if you're a man you can drink up to three bottles a week, and if you're a woman only two.

The council offers further guidance: on any one drinking occasion, men should limit themselves to six standard drinks, and women to four. It should also be remembered that most wines today carry around 14 percent alcohol, whereas these calculations are based on wine with only 12 percent.

In Victorian England, although there was widespread public concern about the ravages of alcoholism, wine was not always seen as a villain. Prime minister William Gladstone openly declared it to be the wise drinking option, a foil for the addictive evil of gin. He had a point: wine is absorbed at a slow, even rate by the blood; spirits, by contrast, rush in and raise blood alcohol to a higher level, albeit for a shorter time.

Put together all of wine's qualities – including its taste, its suitability as a companion for food, and its vaunted medicinal benefits – and its status as the West's most popular drug comes as no surprise.

For a brief spell in the 1840s, French poet Charles Baudelaire and other artistic notables attended the gatherings of Le Club des Hachichins (the Hashish Club) on the Île St Louis in the middle of Paris. Baudelaire was a lover of good wine – Rhine Rieslings were a favourite – but also open to any other stimulant on offer. He probably used hashish only a few times, but unabashedly compared the two intoxicants in his 1860 book *Les Paradis Artificiels*.

'Wine,' he wrote, 'exalts the will, hashish annihilates it. Wine is a support to the body, hashish a weapon for suicide. Wine makes people good and friendly. Hashish isolates. One is hard-working, so to speak, whereas the other is essentially lazy.

'Why would anyone bother to work, to plough, to write, to make anything at all, when with one blow he can attain paradise? Wine is for those people who work and deserve to drink it.'

Wine is at the head of all medicines; where wine is lacking, drugs are necessary.

The Babylonian Talmud
(Hebrew teachings)

Patching up
gladiators

SOMETHING THE EUROPEANS had known for centuries, the Americans discovered — via television, of course — in 1991. A programme that aired on prime time across the United States discussed the 'French paradox' — the apparent capacity of French people to eat and drink to ... well, to their hearts' content. They never seemed to have to pay for it in coronary wards or worse. Red wine was identified as the miracle-worker.

Across the States there was an unprecedented rush on red wine. All types were tried but many didn't meet with the approval of the American palate. One that did was Merlot, the soft, low-acid variety used mostly to give roundness to Bordeaux blends. 'Merlot mania' was born and Californian wineries couldn't pump out the varietal fast enough. We can only wonder how many American hearts were saved from attack by Merlot ingestion.

Wine's most basic, and probably longest-appreciated, virtue for health is its relative safety. You can't catch anything from a glass of wine: thanks to its alcohol and acidity levels, no known human pathogenic bacteria can survive in it. At various times and places in history, this has made wine a safer bet than water. Water was often mixed with wine for no other reason than to make the water safe.

Wine's sterility makes it a useful antiseptic. This property was identified by the famous surgeon Galen, who lived from 120 to 200 AD, during the heyday of the Roman Empire, and influenced the course of medicine for the next 15 centuries. Galen learned his trade patching up gladiators at Pergamon, an outpost of the empire in Asia Minor. When confronted with a gaping wound backstage at the arena, he would immediately apply wine. His boast was that no gladiator had ever died during his watch, a claim some modern scholars find hard to believe.

Throughout the Middle Ages and right up until the late nineteenth century, wine was regularly prescribed by doctors all over Europe for a range of illnesses. The perceived medicinal powers of some varieties enjoyed a particularly strong reputation. An example is Hungary's Tokaji Essenzcia, an extraordinary drink made from botrytis-infected grapes. *Botrytis cinerea*, also known as noble rot, is a fungus that helps create the most delectable, concentrated and mysterious sweet white wines on the planet. Essenczia is obtained when the natural downward pressure of vats full of the withered, botrytis-battered berries releases small quantities of a sweet concentrated amber fluid. It is low in alcohol and almost overwhelmingly rich.

From early times, people from all over Europe were in awe of this wine. Alchemists are said to have taken to Tokaj hill, where the grapes grew, with pickaxes, sure that real gold must be at the root of the vines. The wine's scarceness enhanced its mystery. The aristocracy regarded it as an all-purpose restorative elixir, and credited it with a multitude of miraculous recoveries. Its ability to improve a male's sexual performance to this day remains legendary. When I was visiting Hungary's wine regions a few yeas ago, both Essenczia and its cousin the dessert wine Tokaji Aszu were sometimes referred to as 'Hungarian Viagra'. As a Hungarian wine-maker was kind enough to slip me a small flask, I should be in a position to pass on a personal assessment. Tragically though, despite extremely careful packing, the flask broke on my journey home.

Unsurprisingly, it was the Victorians who started to put the kibosh on the wine-is-healthy school of thought.

Temperance societies sprang up. Where was the proof? they asked. Scientific thought had gained currency and wine's reputation as a health drink was largely anecdotal. The effects of overindulgence began to be studied and alcoholism was, for the first time, defined as a disease. It's taken until now for the wine drinkers of the world to emerge from that dismal era, helped by a wave of scientific evidence supporting wine's health-enhancing properties.

The most widely trumpeted of these, as the Americans learned, is the power of wine to protect against heart disease. Alcohol consumption helps raise the level in the bloodstream of HDL (so-called 'good' cholesterol), which has an anticoagulant effect. Red wine goes further, thanks to the properties of a molecule called resveratrol. Present in the grape skin as a natural protection against fungal infection, resveratrol is shaping up as red wine's magic bullet. Laboratory tests have demonstrated an impressive list of health benefits, including lowering of blood pressure, thinning of blood, and cancer prevention.

Prudent wine consumption can also assist with diabetes, stomach ulcers and anaemia. And a 1998 study found that moderate wine drinkers were less susceptible to sight loss through macular degeneration than non-drinkers.

There is zero fat in wine. This does not, of course, mean it is calorie-free. Wine has calories aplenty, most coming courtesy of the alcohol content. One thing wine is not is a slimmer's drink.

Wine is also redolent in various useful vitamins and minerals, including calcium and potassium. A famous French drinking song contains the line *La vitamine comme ça* (This is how we take our vitamins), with a generous draught of wine the accompanying action.

In America, the government has seen fit to put warnings on wine labels, advising pregnant women to abstain and people in charge of machinery to go softly. The New Zealand government is considering adopting a similar stance.

In the meantime, belief in the positive effects of a moderate wine intake has led several producers in New Zealand to go the other way and decorate their literature with what could be described as health 'appreciations'. Typical is the message on every tasting note of Canterbury winery Pegasus Bay: 'Wine is a natural health food'. Perhaps one day we'll see official signs swinging above wine-bar doors: 'Opened for health reasons'.

You can call a

wine red, and

dry, and strong,

and pleasant.

After that,

Kingsley Amis *watch out . . .*

Words
of mouth

I N THE BOTTOM drawer of my desk there's a file containing a rough outline for a novel, the working title of which is *The Wine Writer*. It's about a newspaper hack, a shocking pisshead, who starts penning a wine column for the provincial daily where he works. It turns out he has a terrific nose, and contrary to all expectations he sobers up and gets serious about his new role. The local wine producers are suddenly forced to treat him respectfully. His influence begins to spread. A local French wine-maker, whose wife is both beautiful and — shall we say — restless, has a guilty secret... Enough, enough — I've already told you far too much.

The novel began as jottings at tastings I attended. Such events never fail to remind me what a strange lark wine-writing is. They invariably throw up diverting nuggets that glow with the allure of fiction.

A few months ago, for example, at the end of a lunch hosted by a producer eagerly introducing his wares to a group of Wellington-based wine writers, gout emerged as a conversation topic. The brows of a couple of older scribes furrowed.

'By Jove, you know when you've got it,' said one. 'Hurts like buggery.'

Some younger writers looked concerned – eager to know the cause of what they now saw as an occupational thundercloud gathering above their heads. Was it Hawke's Bay Claret? Big red Aussie battleships? Too much of everything?

'Scallops,' declared one member of the old guard.

'My medication,' added the other.

We breathed a sigh of relief and returned to the deep, well-made Hawke's Bay Syrah.

Wine writing may be a parasitical activity, as British wine writer Jancis Robinson has observed, but we are a blessed wee swarm of parasites. We indulge regularly in one of life's sensual pleasures, and get paid for it. And in most cases the host beast is all too glad of our dependency.

In New Zealand, the relationship between the wine media and the industry is mostly friendly. Maybe too friendly, some argue, and there is truth in that. But it's not hard to see why it's so. The country has been making reasonable quantities of serious wine for only the past 25 years or so. The astonishing progress over that time has been achieved with the help of a spirit of cooperation and knowledge-sharing among producers.

When a group of New Zealanders pull together and achieve global success in any field, you hear about it. When it comes to getting in behind its own, the local wine media is no exception. (As an aside, an often-cited reason for the pre-eminence of British wine writers is the neutrality that comes with not having a significant local wine industry.)

But what New Zealand lacks is depth of expertise. Wine writing here is a young specialty. When it expanded rapidly over the past decade, there was no large pool of ready-made experience and knowledge to draw on.

With some notable exceptions, most of us are part-timers — often journalists who are also enthusiastic *amateurs de vin* (both the French and English meanings of the word 'amateur' apply) and who pestered an editor until he or she relented and gave us a column. We probably had a measure of confidence in our palates to begin with, but we've had to learn a lot on the job. To tell a wine's story, even superficially, you need to know and understand something about what goes on in the vineyard and the winery.

One of the reasons I began writing about wine was the opportunity it offered me to learn. On my 40th birthday I vowed to try something new every year. These had to be things that exercised the mind, little adventures in self-improvement. The resolution kicked off with enrolment in a Chinese language course at Victoria University. That was literally character-building, because all I remember now is a handful of Mandarin characters. The following year I was offered the wine column at *Capital Times*, Wellington's arts and entertainment weekly. For seven years the column rolled over as the 'new thing' for the following year. I kept telling myself there was still so much to learn.

The New Zealand wine-writing scene generally is not conducive to inquisitive journalism – the kind that can unleash a scandal. But investigative stories haven't been entirely absent. Several years ago *Listener* columnist Keith Stewart broke a story that shook the New Zealand wine industry. Two years after the event, he discovered records proving that west Auckland winery Cooper's Creek had produced and sold a wine that was not true to label. In New Zealand, a varietal wine – that is, one carrying the name of a single variety – must be composed of at least 75 percent of that grape. A Chardonnay that Cooper's Creek's had made for Tesco supermarkets in the United Kingdom, and which had gone on sale as 'Tesco's New Zealand Chardonnay', had dipped well below that.

Vintage records revealed that the Tesco's Chardonnay had been the designated 'ultimate destination' wine for

far more Müller Thurgau, Chasselas and other bulk
varieties than its 5,000 cases could possibly absorb and
still meet the legal definition of Chardonnay.

The story received a lot of coverage. Emerging with
red faces were not just Cooper's Creek and its wine-
making team, but also Tesco, which had sent out an
'international quality standards inspector' at vintage
time. It also showed how reliant the industry was on self-
regulation. Stewart felt he had no choice but to go public
with the story, but at the same time it saddened him. He
knew the integrity of most of the industry was beyond
reproach. He particularly felt for 'all the little guys with
dreams' whose efforts could be compromised by a bigger
company's transgression.

'You never write anything bad about the wines you
review,' I'm sometimes told. That's true, mostly. I tend
to recommend what I enjoy, rather than list wines that
have disappointed me. The unpalatable – and today
there are few New Zealand wines in this category –
remain unnoted.

I always approach a wine from a standpoint of
respect. In most cases, a wine-maker has poured heart
and soul into the bottle. I doubt there is a wine writer
in the world who has not socialised with a wine producer. And of course their product is a social lubricant.
Inevitably, friendships are made. But when you're
reviewing, you must forget that in his cellar a wine-
maker once described his wines to you as his children.

One path to neutrality favoured by a number of writers is to blind-taste everything that comes for review. At certain times of the year my front door is the repository of a constant stream of snow-white polystyrene slabs encasing wine bottles. There's no possibility of publishing reviews of all these wines without writing shopping-list style columns devoid of the industry's informative, diverting tales. But I make sure I taste them all and note the results in my wine journal, a necessary companion for any wine writer.

The words we wine writers use to describe specific wines are the constant butt of ridicule. 'Were you three sheets to the wind when you wrote that?' is a typical jibe. The problem is that we are always groping for words where there are none. Any written description of a wine will go only so far towards informing a reader what the wine is really like – its smell, its taste, its texture.

Things can become particularly tricky with less complex varietals such as Sauvignon Blanc. 'It is aromatic, with fresh, strong, ripely herbaceous flavours, showing good delicacy and purity, and a smooth finish.' That's a description plucked at random from a New Zealand wine book. It's fair to say a lot of sauvignons could claim the same description. A wine's individuality and special charms can only really be understood when it is tasted.

Smell and taste are excessively difficult things to convey. They're like colours. How do you describe red to someone? Inevitably you reach for comparisons ... lipstick, fire engines, pohutukawa flowers. Similarly, wine reviews and tasting notes are often jungles of metaphor and simile.

In defence of these comparisons, in many cases 'comparison' is the wrong word. Wine is one of the most complex-tasting of foods, host to thousands of flavour compounds. Many of these are shared with all sorts of other foods and plant life. When you think you are smelling black olives in a wine, you may well be. The chemical make-up for both can be the same.

Making verbal connections to smells is also problematic. Unlike other senses, the nose needs more than words to recall a smell clearly. We instantly recognise a known smell. The smells of childhood, for instance, are famously evocative. For me, a whiff of new-mown grass never fails to trip off a cascade of images of sunny family Saturdays.

But simply receiving a verbal prompt is a different matter. If someone were to describe a piece of music to you as being very like the theme to *Mission: Impossible*, you'd immediately have a strong idea of what they meant. The same is true with a visual image. If you were told someone looked like Michael Jackson, you'd know the person was skinny, pasty-faced, had long black hair and a very odd nose. But if you're told something smells like boiled cabbage, even though you've probably smelled boiled cabbage hundreds of times in your life you can probably conjure up only a vague sensory memory.

These matters may soon be rendered irrelevant if the situation in Britain is anything to go by. There, wine writers are starting to look like an endangered species. A number of dailies and magazines have dropped their wine columns completely, while others live on in reduced circumstances. There are currently no wine programmes on British television; there were several a decade ago.

One of the reasons is advertising, or rather the lack of it. The accountants attached to media operations have a keen nose for journalism that generates advertising, which explains why every newspaper has a motoring columnist. Wine companies are not huge spenders on advertising, and in most countries television advertising of alcohol is either restricted or banned.

A branch of wine information that hasn't suffered is the buyers' guide. Consumers, it seems, are particularly keen to catch someone's opinion on what's hot, and what's cheap. Price is crucial information for a wine writer to pass on. The reader needs to know if buying the object of effusive praise will be financially injurious. Wine, like art and jewellery, is a meeting place for fashion, snobbery, rarity, 'expert opinion', investment, subjectivity and silly money, which can make for some distorted pricing.

There are many reasons a $100 bottle of wine might be so priced, the underlying one being that someone, somewhere, is probably willing to pay that amount for it. You can be sure of one thing: it won't be five times better than a good $20 bottle. The higher you go in price, the smaller the differences in quality become, and the more the 'trophy wine syndrome' comes into play. You pay extra to be seen with a wine brand to be seen with.

Rest assured you can drink very good wine and pay no more than $15 to $20. That's as it should be, an affordable pleasure. And I never tire of trotting out this cliché: a good wine is a wine you enjoy.

I don't give a shit that your family goes back to pre-Revolution and you've got more wealth than I could imagine. If this wine's no good, **Robert Parker, Jr** *I'm going to say so.*

Unsettling scores

I N THE UNLIKELY locale of Monkton, Maryland lives one of the wine world's most powerful men. On most mornings Robert Parker, Jr will enter an office in his house and shoo out the old labrador. Next, he will start tasting wines.

He tastes fine wines from all around the globe, including New Zealand, although the wines of France have long held a special attraction for him. He pours the wine himself and tastes it standing up, which he says helps him stay focussed. He either writes notes, or records his impressions on a small tape recorder. And he scores each of the 10,000 wines he tastes every year out of 100.

Parker established his reputation with the 1982 Bordeaux vintage, when he ran against the critical tide, predicting it would be a great vintage, and was proved correct. What his numbers have done since then is nothing short of extraordinary. For legions of consumers around the world, these scores have become the gospel. A high Parker score is, therefore, the best marketing tool a producer can hope for. A low score can be ruinous.

No one doubts that Parker's palate is remarkably consistent and well-honed, and that he is independent and incorruptible. He never accepts free samples, pays his own way everywhere, doesn't invest in wine futures, and seldom socialises with producers. And yet for the French wine establishment, particularly in Bordeaux and Burgundy, he is an American Satan. The most astonishing effect of the power his scores wield is that many French producers, resentfully but quietly, have begun making wines to suit his palate.

The kinds of wines Parker prefers are big and dark, rich in fruit and alcohol. He has admitted a personal fondness for the reds of the southern Rhône. For the old guard at Bordeaux, who have always maintained that their forte is subtlety, finesse and wines that don't come into their own for decades, the idea of an outsider dictating terms has been anathema. At one Bordeaux chateau whose vintage had been poorly reviewed by Parker, the American was attacked by a dog while the owner stood by and watched.

'Bob is a big dramatic man, with big dramatic tastes,' an influential Bordeaux producer said in a recent interview. 'But our wines are supposed to be red, not black. I will no longer read what he writes. He wants to lead us down a path of destruction.'

Parker shrugs off all of this. In his small-town American way, he wishes he hadn't made such a fuss. But he also sees himself as a plain speaker who is breaking down a tradition of big business wrapped up in pretence, mystique – and bullshit.

Unfortunately for Parker, he will probably not be remembered principally for his remarkable palate or personal integrity, but for the most limited, imperfect and awkward aspect of his work: his scoring system.

Wine competitions and critics bestowed rankings on wine (often using the less brutal 1 to 5 stars treatment) before Parker, but he was the first to use the 100-point approach. His success has caused wine-scoring to spread like a rumour. Now, everybody's doing it.

Each year I bring together a tasting panel that works its way through the spring releases of Wairarapa wineries. We blind-taste around 100 wines and score them out of 20. The results – words and scores – are compiled and published. The event is fun. It gives me an early and comprehensive glimpse of our local wine region's vintage. And its scale is modest, which suits me. To avoid palate fatigue, we taste around 25 wines a day over four days. Tasting over 100 a day, as judges do in some wine competitions, would not be my idea of a pleasant vinous experience.

So the Wairarapa wine-tasting is all good – except for one nagging, central discomfort: attaching a number to a glass of wine feels crass. Most wine critics share this misgiving. One of the reasons wine is talked and written about so much is its ethereal, elusive nature. Wine defies certainty, yet a number is by definition a certainty. The old Latin proverb 'De gustibus solum est disputandum' – 'Only matters of taste are worth arguing over' – quickly falls by the wayside when something as absolute as a number is applied.

Taste is inescapably subjective. One person's five-star wine might be lucky to get three stars from someone else. On my own tasting panel there have been strong disagreements among experienced tasters. When there's a divergence of views, things gets muddy. When the scores are averaged out, you can end up with a figure that offers few clues about the wine. With a lone operator such as Robert Parker, you can at least decide whether or not you concur with his palate and, if so, follow it.

Consistency is another problem. Your personal state of mind, influenced by mood, surroundings and company, will have much to do with how you score a wine. You can taste the same wine a few days apart and mark it quite differently.

Tasting a big line-up is also difficult. Big showy wines stand out from the crowd and demand attention, especially when judges' palates are becoming frayed. Subtlety, a virtue in wine, is often not rewarded in such a forum.

And then there is the undue influence that scores carry. Parker is an extreme example, but every time a wine critic – any wine critic – promulgates a score, it can become opinion-forming. So why do we keep scoring? Because so many wine drinkers are unconfident around wine. They want reassurance and something tangible to guide them. A number is easily understood. Ergo, publications with wine scores sell.

Parker is well aware of the monster he has helped create but shows no remorse. He sees himself as a simple consumer advocate, a man with opinions who is not afraid to express them. And just in case the worst should happen, a few years ago he insured his nose for a million dollars.

New Zealand may produce only 0.79 percent of the world's vino, but it has achieved the near miraculous feat of persuading us Brits to spend more than £5 on a bottle.

Tim Atkin,
The Observer

Wine à la mode

I N 1905 A NEW ZEALAND rugby team captivated the United Kingdom with the fluid skill and diligence of its play, and the guileless natural charm of its players. By the end of its seven-month tour, the side had become the darlings of the old country. They had also established a brand: the All Blacks.

In 1982, a clutch of Marlborough wine-makers jumped on a plane to give London a taste of their new Sauvignon Blancs, which they felt quite pleased about. It was to be a repeat of 1905, only with wine. A shared purity of product and people won over a gathering largely made up of wine merchants and members of the influential British wine press. Accustomed to tastings fronted by guarded, jaded European producers, the guests left New Zealand House refreshed in every sense.

That tasting, held nearly 150 years after the country's first wine had been made by official British Resident James Busby at Waitangi, would turn out to be a spark igniting an international New Zealand wine phenomenon.

There had previously been small ascendant moments, such as the comments made by French writer and connoisseur André Simon on a 1964 visit. Given a 1949 McDonald Hawke's Bay Cabernet Sauvignon to taste alongside a Château Margaux of the same vintage, Simon had noted, 'It [the Margaux] did not shame the New Zealand cousin of the same vintage.' The local wine was, he said, 'rare and convincing proof that New Zealand can bring forth table wines of a very high standard.'

By the mid 1980s, the British market was locking on to Marlborough Sauvignon Blanc with almost religious fervour. The New Zealanders' timing had been excellent. For years British light white wine drinkers had been suffering watery French Muscadets and Italian Frascatis. Marlborough had suddenly offered an arresting, affordable new white wine experience unmatched at that time.

Through a mixture of design and good fortune, Marlborough Sauvignon Blanc became an established and crucial brand. Before we knew it, New Zealand had cornered one of the world's classic grape varieties in several key markets. A chief reason was the New World wine-makers' habit of identifying wine on labels principally by grape variety. In Sauvignon Blanc's home territories, Sancerre and Pouilly Fumé in the Loire, it's not called Sauvignon Blanc; it's called Sancerre and Pouilly Fumé. Only wine buffs know that, certainly not most of the people in English-speaking markets who develop a taste for the variety. They just know they like Sauvignon Blanc and that New Zealand leads the pack. New Zealand's Sauvignon Blanc producers have fortuitously avoided going head to head with those who are potentially their strongest competitors.

Marlborough Sauvignon Blanc became a hothouse in which a cluster of individual brands flourished. Cloudy Bay in particular, with its evocative name (copywriter: Capt Jas. Cook) and labels, backed by the quality of the wine, spawned a cult following. It remains one of the most distinctive winery brands in the world.

New Zealand wine's rise has been a story of giddy — almost outrageous — growth and success. Since 1987, an average of 20 new wineries have materialised each year. Vineyard plantings across the country have nearly quadrupled in size since 1982 to over 18,000 hectares. Marlborough's Wairau plain, now largely devoid of sheep and cattle, can be described as a monoculture.

Increasing amounts of the liquid bounty of these vines goes offshore, for New Zealanders are still drinking roughly the same amount of local wine they were 20 years ago. (Imports, mainly from Australia, have been taking over bulk wine shelves in supermarkets, and the local industry has wisely concentrated on producing a more distinctive product.)

In 2004, New Zealand wine exports reached 31 million litres, compared to a mere half a million in 1982. International interest, praise and competition success have become commonplace. Today, the industry is an established source of national pride and pleasure. There were nods of approval all round when George Fistonich, pioneer wine producer and godfather of New Zealand's largest family-owned winery, Villa Maria, was in 2005 awarded one of the country's highest honours, Distinguished Companion of the New Zealand Order of Merit.

Small things remind me how globally significant New Zealand wine has become. I recently read a short story in *The New Yorker* by Pulitzer Prize-winning novelist Richard Ford. In it, real estate agent Frank Bascombe, Ford's best known literary hero (*The Sportswriter*, *Independence Day*), is having lunch with a client, during which they enjoy a bottle of 'New Zealand Gewürztraminer'. Bascombe may be a fictional character, but it's still a hell of a product endorsement.

New Zealand wine's new status is apparent, too, on visits to other wine-producing countries. I once sat tasting wine in a cellar in Hungary, aware of the wronged, accusatory gaze of a wizened Magyar at the other end of the table. Eventually he blurted out, 'You New Zealanders and your Sauvignon Blanc! What is this? How?'

I understood his mystification. He was producing wine in the same place his ancestors had for centuries. Every secret the land and vines had ever held had been surrendered to his family over that time. Yet while the lights never seemed to stop turning green for New Zealand wine, he was having difficulty selling his carefully crafted product. With a typical kiwi eagerness to restore *bonhomie*, I hastily replied, 'Well, things can change quickly. At home, all the talk now is of Pinot Gris.' This seemed only to trouble and perplex him more.

A couple of years later I was in the Rheingau in Germany, drinking tea on the terrace of Dr Franz Michel's beautiful house. As his grandchildren played in the vines that sloped down towards the Rhine, the former president of the German Wine Institute gave me a wry look. 'I was in New Zealand once, 20 years ago,' he remarked. 'Only for a couple of days, which I spent in court. Montana had called one of its wines Bernkästler Riesling and we had to put a stop to that. But … a lot has changed since then, hein?'

Yes, things can, and do, change quickly. And as we are often told, wine is beholden to the whims of fashion. This can be particularly true for white wines, which perfectly fit the role of quaffable stand-alone trendy bar and party drinks. There is frequent discussion in New Zealand wine circles about the fact Sauvignon Blanc accounts for two-thirds of our exports. Diversification and promoting other wines is seen as wise insurance against the dread possibility that the sauvignon bubble will one day burst.

Yet if Sauvignon Blanc's success is mainly about fashion, twenty years is an enviably long fashion statement. And rather than block out the sun, the white wine's ebullient presence has helped create interest in other New Zealand wines. During the late 1980s, serious Bordeaux blends and Syrahs began emerging from Hawke's Bay. Further south, the first Martinborough Pinot Noirs appeared. These excellent reds, and the 3.5 million litres of Chardonnay that New Zealand exports each year, would have found the international going much tougher had there been no Sauvignon Blanc delirium.

Montana's sparkling wine Lindauer also offers evidence of the opportunities that exist beyond Sauvignon Blanc. When Lindauer was created by Montana in 1981 it was something of a gamble: a wine made according to champagne's *méthode traditionelle* but priced as low as margins would allow. Initial sales were good, but not stunning. That all changed in 1990, when Lindauer won International Sparkling Wine of the Year at the London Wine Challenge.

Four million bottles of Lindauer are now produced every year. One million are sold in Britain, where the wine is even better known than in New Zealand and the price seldom dips below £8 (NZ$21). At home, New

Zealand supermarket shoppers spend more money on Lindauer each December than on any other single product. Lindauer has become the single biggest-selling New Zealand wine of all time.

What makes New Zealand so good at producing wine? Looking at the map and comparing the latitudes of our wine regions with those in Europe – a talking point in the 1970s – is largely pointless. For example, we regard the Central Otago region as being 'on the edge' viticulturally. And yet the Rheingau in Germany, if its latitude were translated to the southern hemisphere, would share a position with the frozen Antipodes Islands, 643 kilometres south-east of Bluff. Different weather patterns, such as the Gulf Stream that crosses the Atlantic to Europe, make these comparisons meaningless.

New Zealand's key natural attribute is the same thing that makes its seafood so tasty: the climate. If you've ever eaten fish caught in the tropics, you'll know it rarely has the intense, vigorous taste of fish caught in temperate zones. Life for everybody and everything can be draining in the heat. Grapes certainly need sun to ripen, but too much sun can kill acids and elevate sugar levels. The result is big, loud, unbalanced wines, high in alcohol but low in elegance and flavour nuance.

A cool climate like New Zealand's will never bake grapes, and some years a number of varieties will struggle even to ripen. Much of the time, though, it will deliver fruit capable of making wines with depth of flavour and real finesse. To a Frenchman, our wines taste too *fruité*. To the new young wine drinker in London or Sydney or New York, they taste rewardingly clean and bright.

Thanks mainly to the many small artisan producers who have been responsible for establishing its reputation, New Zealand is cleverly positioned at the quality end of the international market. It has the highest per-litre value of any wine-exporting country in the world.

New Zealand's other big asset is its people. Unlike most European wine producers, our wine-makers did not inherit their land and jobs. They chose to chase a dream. Most have invested heavily in their businesses, making them doubly hungry. They're driven to learn all they can, and produce the best wine they can.

In the early 1980s they did this any way they could. One delightful story that has passed into legend is the arrival of the 'gumboot clone'. In the mid '70s a vine cutting was discovered at Auckland Airport in the gumboot of a New Zealander returning from overseas. The cutting – or 'clone' in wine parlance – chose its customs officer well. On duty that day was Malcolm Abel, who in his spare time was establishing a vineyard at Henderson. He was very interested in what he found in the gumboot. Abel quizzed the would-be importer, who informed him it was a Pinot Noir clone. And not just any pinot clone: it had apparently been obtained from Burgundy's celebrated La Tâche vineyard, when the man had shinned over a stone wall and helped himself to a cutting.

The clone was confiscated, as required by law, but mysteriously sidestepped quarantine. Instead Abel planted it in Henderson, and was very pleased with the results. He died prematurely in 1981, but prior to that he passed a cutting on to his friend Clive Paton, who was establishing Ata Rangi winery in pinot-friendly Martinborough.

A mixture of different clones is important in the making of great Pinot Noir. Ata Rangi's world-renowned pinot today owes about a third of its content to the gumboot clone, which is now widely planted throughout Martinborough and is spreading into the South Island's pinot regions as well.

This is a good example of the cooperative approach taken by New Zealand's wine producers. Another is the way in which, at the end of every vintage, the producers of Otago Pinot Noir send samples of their new wine to their counterparts in Martinborough, who all get together to taste it and later return the favour. If this kind of *ésprit collectif* ever existed in the Old World, it was lost centuries ago.

The pioneering days are over. Many wine-makers have grown wealthy over the last two decades. The industry has been an economic dynamo, lighting up tracts of hitherto quiet, and in some cases depressed, rural hinterland. Not everyone in these areas is enamoured of the new crop. In Martinborough, residents banded together in 2003 to sign a petition protesting against the noise created by the 20 helicopters the wine-producers brought in one night to combat the frost. Yet even the aggrieved can't dispute that the wine industry employs thousands of people, and in many cases has caused the value of their own land to rise astronomically.

And industry economics spread well beyond the wine regions themselves. In Wellington, John Follas makes a living storing wine for hundreds of clients in his carefully calibrated mid-city cellar. A young New Zealander in London, Martin Brown, has created www.winesearcher.com, one of the most visited wine sites on the internet.

We now have a wine culture in New Zealand. While it becomes more entrenched by the year, it still overexcites and overawes us. We are forever prodding it, wallowing in it, worrying about it, complicating it. Jasper Morris, a British wine merchant, remarked at the Pinot Noir 2004 conference in Wellington: 'New Zealand [wine people] are over-fearful. Great New Zealand Pinot Noir will come when people worry less and relax more. You need to go with the flow. *Il faut avoir le courage de ne rien faire.* You must be brave enough to do nothing.'

Inevitably, as the thrill and novelty of being a wine country fades, that will happen. We will learn to live more calmly alongside wine. Yet there's only so much nonchalance and lack of wonder you can maintain. Wine will be constantly celebrated. For the many ways it makes us happy, for the power it has to connect us to people and places and for the alchemy at the centre of its creation, wine will always be something the world can't keep quiet about.

ACKNOWLEDGEMENTS

A number of people have assisted me in the writing of this book and deserve heartfelt thanks. Roger Parkinson of Nga Waka Vineyard placed his deep reservoir of technical knowledge at my disposal and for that I'm grateful. Keith Stewart also took time to read and comment on the manuscript. And finally my wife, Rolla, had input in any number of supportive ways.

I would also like to acknowledge the following key information sources: Michael Cooper, *Wine Atlas of New Zealand* (Hodder Moa Beckett, 2002); Hugh Johnson, *The Story of Wine* (Mitchell Beazley, 1989); Hugh Johnson, *Wine* (Mitchell Beazley, 1974); A.J. Liebling, *Between Meals: An Appetite For Paris* (Modern Library, 1959); William Langewiesche, 'The Million Dollar Nose' published in *The Best American Magazine Writing 2001* (PublicAffairs, 2001); Jancis Robinson (ed.), *The Oxford Companion to Wine* (Oxford University Press, 1994); Edmund White, *The Flâneur: A Stroll Through the Paradoxes of Paris* (Bloomsbury, 2001).